PLANT

Julia A. Royston

BK Royston Publishing
Jeffersonville, IN 47131
http://www.bkroystonpublishing.com
bkroystonpublishing@gmail.com

ISBN-13: 978-1-971868-30-1

King James Version (KJV) – Public Domain

Printed in the United States of America

Dedication

To all that only want to Plant, Be Planted and Rooted in God's Will and Plan for Your Life.

Theme Scripture

“I have planted, Apollos watered; but God gave the increase.”

1 Corinthians 3:6 (KJV)

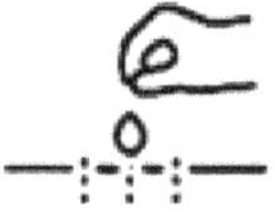

Acknowledgements

I thank my Lord and Savior Jesus Christ for giving me another opportunity to introduce more people to you. I thank you for entrusting this gift to me. Lord, let your Spirit move, guide and empower through this book to the people who will read it.

To my husband, Brian K. Royston, the love of my life, for loving and cheering me on so much that I can be and do all that God has placed in me. I love you.

To my mom, my greatest supporter and best friend. To my dad, who is in Heaven, who I know is proud of me and always encouraged me to go for it. Thanks to all the rest of my family for their love and support.

A special thank you to Rev. and Mrs. Claude R. Royston for their love and support.

To the rest of my clients, friends and family, thank you and love you always.

Let's go!

Table of Contents

Introduction

As God has inspired me to write many times, this series is no different. From ASK, SEEK and KNOCK, to Plant, Water and Increase.

Whatever He is telling you to do, do it. Whatever He has placed on your heart or you are inspired to do, do it.

Whatsoever a man or woman or boy or girl doeth, shall prosper. It's time to get our hands dirty, get the seeds and PLANT.

Let's go!

Planted By God Himself

And the Lord God **plant**ed a garden eastward in Eden; and there he put the man whom he had formed. Genesis 2:8 (KJV)

The creator Himself planted the first thing. He planted a garden in Eden. He made the decision. He created the seed that would actually go in the ground. He determined what that seed would produce. This time, right here, He actually did the planting. The scripture doesn't say that He spoke or that He thought it and it happened. In this particular place, time, and event, He did the planting. God is a spirit and thus how He did the planting remains a mystery, but we know that with creating man, He got His hands dirty. So maybe God got His hands dirty while planting the garden. However it was done, it was curated carefully, with Adam and eventually Eve in mind.

My grandmother had a garden. She decided what would go in it. She bought the seeds. She turned the soil. She fought back the bugs and anything else that would harm her harvest. She picked the harvest, cooked the harvest and served the harvest to anyone that came to the house.

Planting the garden yourself is only the beginning but knowing that God, the creator of the earth planted the garden, tells me to get my plate, knife and fork because there will be an abundance and we will have plenty to eat.

Prayer:

Lord, I thank YOU that YOU planted me. In Jesus' name. Amen.

NOTES

NOTES

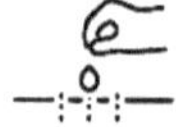

Plant Them in the Mountain

Thou shalt bring them in, and plant them in the mountain of thine inheritance, in the place, O Lord, which thou hast made for thee to dwell in, in the Sanctuary, O Lord, which thy hands have established.

Exodus 15:17 (KJV)

Anything or anyone that is planted in the mountains must be strong, tough and capable of enduring the terrain and soil of the mountains. If something is sitting on the side of the road, near the highway or any other easily accessible street, it gives your harvest the ability to be stolen quickly and easily.

Travelling through South Carolina, cotton fields were not even 10 feet from the road. Trespassing was unnecessary. It was so easy to pull over with hazard lights and take pictures of the white cotton still in the fields.

Now being planted on a mountain is no easy feat. Why? Mountains require a lot of effort. If there is no road that has been tediously plowed and created through the mountain, I'm not a mountain climber.

Being planted in the mountains is a great place to be because we are high enough for the elements to grow but far enough away to make it hard for the enemy to steal or gain access.

Prayer:

God, I thank YOU that YOU planted me in the mountains. High enough so that I’m never out of your sight but high enough, so that the enemy can’t destroy me.

NOTES

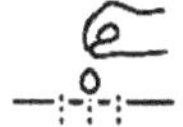

NOTES

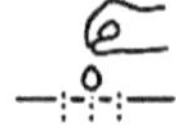

Good Things I Didn't Plant

And houses full of all good things, which thou filledst not, and wells digged, which thou diggedst not, vineyards and olive trees, which thou plantedst not; when thou shalt have eaten and be full;

Deuteronomy 6:11 (KJV)

My parents always taught me to be appreciative. Please, thank you and you're welcome must have been right behind my first words of daddy and mama. I say please and thank you so often that I even say it to myself. It didn't matter about the gift, thought or gesture, I was taught to be eternally grateful.

I don't cook but I love to eat good food. So, if you bring me a plate, I'm good. If you hold the door for me, I'm thankful. If you thought about me in any way, shape or form, I'm grateful.

Now with God, there is so much that we can thank Him for that we really don't have the words. Thank you sometimes just has to suffice.

In this scripture, I could literally stop at the opening clause, a house full of all good things. A house, not a tent, tree or open air covering but a whole house. The house is not only stable but full. Now you can have a house filled with junk, trash, rodents and other horrible things but this house is full of ALL good things.

That's it. That's the entry. Nothing else in that verse needs to be addressed for you to start worshipping, praising and literally running around the room. God did it back then and He WILL do it again.

Prayer:

Thank you God that my house is full of all of the good things. In Jesus' name. Amen.

NOTES

NOTES

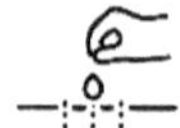

All That Work Planting But I Can't Enjoy It

Thou shalt plant vineyards, and dress them, but shalt neither drink of the wine, nor gather the grapes; for the worms shall eat them.

Deuteronomy 28:39 (KJV)

I don't know why God sometimes does not allow us to reap a harvest, see the fruit of our labor and enjoy the spoils after all of the hard work. Is it our sin? Is it disobedience? Is it pride or arrogance? Maybe it is just God's will and plan for our lives. The children of Israel oftentimes struggled with enjoying the harvest God prepared because of disobedience, sin, murmuring and complaining. Complaining about the work. Complaining about the people. Complaining about 'all of the things.' In those times of complaining, we have to remember that God is listening. Ouch! I needed that one too. He hears not only what we say but also what we think, feel and never say out loud.

Now, I still wouldn't be okay even if I knew who enjoyed the harvest instead of me, but in Deuteronomy, the worms ate it. Now worms are normally on the ground, low to it, or climb high, slowly but surely, to reach their destination. They don't fly. They don't have large feet, but on their belly they crawl one inch at a time. Now imagine that God stopped all of the major, fast moving animals and people from getting the harvest and saved it for the worm. Ouch again!

Prayer:

Lord, help me not to let anything I do or say stop me from enjoying the harvest that you have prepared for me. In Jesus' name. Amen.

NOTES

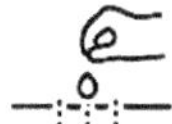

NOTES

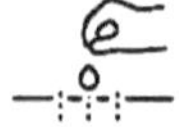

A Gift: Something You Did Not Plant

And I have given you a land for which ye did not labour, and cities which ye built not, and ye dwell in them; of the vineyards and oliveyards which ye planted not do ye eat.

Joshua 24:13 (KJV)

The journey was long. There was a lot of loss on the way to Canaan land for the children of Israel. Only the ones under 21 years of age got to go into the promise land. The grandmothers, great-grandmothers, and even mothers died in the wilderness because of murmuring, complaining, and unbelief. The leader, Joshua was seasoned, experienced and older and knew the ways of God.

The parents and older generation who spent years in Egypt weren't there to compare what once was to where they arrived. God prepared the cities, vineyards, and olive yards so that the people who entered had plenty to eat but didn't have to begin planting.

They enjoyed the hard work of God and those that had been there before they arrived. Their job now was to enjoy the gift of abundance from something that they DID not plant.

Prayer:

God, we thank YOU that YOU are the giver of GOOD gifts. You still do exceedingly and abundantly above that we can even ask or think. In Jesus' name. Amen.

NOTES

NOTES

An Appointed Place

Moreover I will appoint a place for my people Israel, and will plant them, that they may dwell in a place of their own, and move no more; neither shall the children of wickedness afflict them anymore, as beforetime,

2 Samuel 7:10 (KJV)

Elections and voting are tricky. No, I am not being political here but there is a difference between voting for something and being appointed to a specific position. The appointment usually has fewer people, opinions and is more final than if someone is elected and/or there is a vote that takes place. Being appointed to a position may have a time limit, but being appointed is special. You were chosen. You were selected. Deliberation may or may not have taken place. A review of your qualifications, what you bring to the organization and what your future could look like based on your past experience is all considered when you are appointed. We shouldn't take being appointed lightly.

It is an honor. It is a privilege.

God said, "I will." Just the fact that God said that He will do a thing is enough right there for you to start packing, preparing, and positioning yourself for it. He can't lie. Secondly, He said, "I'll appoint a place for my people." Whatever or whoever is there now will be vacating the premises. Finally, He said, "I will plant them." In another scripture, He said, "No man can pluck you out of MY hands." Whatever is in His power to plant, no man will be able to pluck it up. God also said, they will move no more. That's it. It's settled. To this we say Amen.

Prayer:

God, thank you for YOUR appointed place. In Jesus' name. Amen.

NOTES

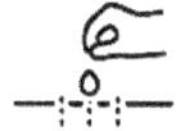

NOTES

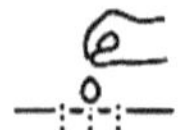

It Takes GOD to Grow What is Planted

And Abraham planted a grove in Beersheba, and called there on the name of the Lord, the everlasting God.

Genesis 21:33 (KJV)

Abraham did the work. He planted the grove in Beersheba but then he went to the one who could actually grow what he planted and that was God. There are times when we do put in the work. We do the homework and research. We buy books and other materials. We go to class, turn in the papers, and pass all of the exams. We start the business. We take all of the business courses, get accepted in the cohort, and do all of the things required, but it is going to take God to grow what you planted.

You need God's favor. You need God's direction. You need God's instruction and

His warning to make sure that you don't lose ground, don't allow the enemy to attack, and don't let him destroy all of your hard work and effort.

It takes God. Don't ever think that you can do it all on your own. Work without God is just energy spent. Work with God is work with an expectation of lasting and fruitful harvest.

Remember it still takes the everlasting God.

Prayer:

Father, We still can do ALL things through Christ. In Jesus' name. Amen.

NOTES

NOTES

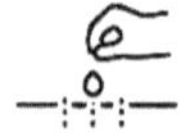

Planted by Water

And he shall be like a tree planted by the rivers of water, that bringeth forth his fruit in his season; his leaf also shall not wither; and whatsoever he doeth shall prosper.

Psalm 1:3 (KJV)

Nothing you plant will die sooner than when there is a drought. Water is essential for anything that you plant. Most civilizations are planted near a major body of water. Transportation, agriculture, food, commerce, business and travel come from water. Cut off the water supply and things will start to wither and eventually die.

As someone who has lived the majority of my life near the Ohio River in Kentucky, I see fun, work, and business thrive on the river.

What if you were planted by water? God said that you shall be like a tree planted by the rivers of water. Not one river, like the Ohio but multiple rivers. There is no lack of what is needed to grow if planted by water. The plants by the water will prosper and so will you.

Prayer:

Lord, plant me by YOUR rivers so that I may prosper. In Jesus' name. Amen.

NOTES

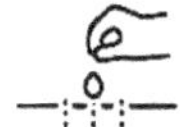

NOTES

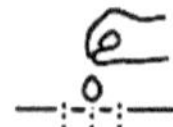

Planted in the Right House

Those that be **plant**ed in the house of the Lord shall flourish in the courts of our God.

Psalm 92:13 (KJV)

When my parents moved my sisters and me from one neighborhood to another, the realtor took them on a house hunt. We really didn't care where we moved, but each of us having our own room was the ultimate goal. Our parents cared where we lived, what schools we went to and who our neighbors were. They wanted the best for us, and they hunted until they found it. My mother still lives there to this day.

The house has needed much maintenance over the years, but we still feel like it is now our house. Our family was planted; we accomplished many things — graduated from college, married our husbands, and saw our family and friends enjoy coming to 'our house.' If you are planted in the house of the Lord, you shall flourish in the courts of our God. I believe that. Is the house where you are planted a house of the Lord, or just a sign on the door? On the other hand, if it is a house of the Lord, why do you resist being planted there? Ouch. My sisters and I didn't always agree with the rules of the house, but we were planted there and didn't leave until it was time to go and build our own houses. Consequently, we were planted and now flourish in God's courts wherever He leads us.

Prayer:

Lord, help me to remain planted in YOUR house and flourish in YOUR courts. In Jesus' name. Amen.

NOTES

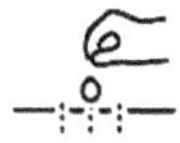

NOTES

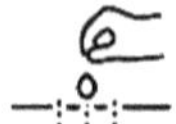

My Ear is Planted to Hear

He that planted the ear, shall he not hear? he that formed the eye, shall he not see?

Psalm 94:9 (KJV)

The best way to get a harvest for crops is to put a seed in the ground. Dirt, mulch and manure are dirty, but it is required to grow a seed to a plant. It doesn't always have a pleasant smell, but it is good for seeds. It's great for growth. Add some water and sunlight on top, and you have a making of a bumper crop.

But where should your ear be planted to best hear? As a child who suffered from allergies and chronic and excess wax in my ears, I failed many hearing tests. The trips to the ear, nose and throat doctor were prevalent and still are to this day. Ears don't function best in dirt. Ears filled with wax that clogs, or water that doesn't allow the ear canal to hear best, are not desired.

The ear should be planted in truth. The ear that is planted in a powerful, consistent, and pure connection to God, His word, and His ways hears best.

Just as the farmer is very careful where he plants his seeds, tests out the soil, and fights off any attacks that can stop growth, the same should be true for your ears. Let God plant your ear so that you can hear, obey and move forward in the way that He would have you go in your life.

Prayer:

Lord, plant my ear in YOUR truth. In Jesus' name. Amen.

NOTES

NOTES

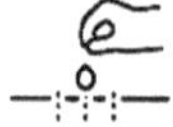

Planted Children Round About

Thy wife shall be as a fruitful vine by the sides of thine house: thy children like olive plants round about thy table.

Psalm 128:3 (KJV)

Accumulating things is normally a sign of wealth, income and independence. The land, houses, cars and money usually equal wealth. In ancient times, it was no different. Land, cattle, sheep, oxen and any tangible coin, gold or silver was a sign of wealth. For a woman in ancient times, her wealth, importance, and stature were connected to having children.

When Hannah was not able to bear children, she fasted, prayed and petitioned the Lord for a child and not just a child but a man child, boy, heir to her husband's wealth and he would be a leader for the next generation. A son would take care of not only his father's house but his own house, and secure and maintain a future for his mother and any other siblings. It was important. It was meaningful and for a woman, it was everything. Hannah said, "A child, lest I die." That's how serious it was for her.

The promise in this text is of a fruitful vine and a producing womb. To have children planted in your household was one of the highest blessings and promises from God. If, like me, you have no biological children, I promise you that He WILL bring you godchildren, nieces, nephews, and bonus children to take care of you until the end of your days.

Prayer:

Lord, plant children in my house or in my life like fruitful vines. These children are not only for my care but my legacy. In Jesus' name. Amen.

NOTES

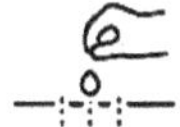

NOTES

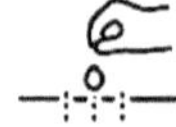

She Planted A Vineyard

She considereth a field, and buyeth it: with the fruit of her hands she planteth a vineyard.

Proverbs 31:16 (KJV)

The Proverbs 31 woman is special. She clearly has God's strength, courage, wisdom, power, stamina and vision. She is still talked about today but has no name. I believe that she is a culmination of multiple women. All women should aspire to find themselves somewhere in chapter 31.

My grandmother planted a garden each and every year until she couldn't do it physically. Gardening is key to eating well, but an even bigger deal to work, tend, maintain, and harvest to the table.

The Proverbs 31 woman didn't just work in the vineyard; she considered the field first. That means she thought about it, weighed her options, analyzed it, determined the worth, and then checked her numbers.

Secondly, she bought it. Now ownership is for the strategic, wealthy, or one with access to means and money to purchase. This situation looks so different when you understand that women weren't supposed to own anything. She not only owned it but made the decision to own it. It wasn't gifted to her; she didn't inherit it — she made the decision and then planted the vineyard. A vineyard is an asset that can be scaled and serve as the foundation for an empire.

What do you want to buy?

Prayer:

Lord, give me strategy and the ability to own and build what you have gifted my head, hands and heart to do. In Jesus' name. Amen.

NOTES

NOTES

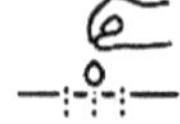

God Let Me Do It!

I made me great works; I builded me houses; I planted me vineyards.

Ecclesiastes 2:4 (KJV)

There are people who only envision the idea or the project. They may write some things down, talk to others about investing, offer some suggestions for improvement, and may even see the early stages of the project, but never get to see the finished work. They go to glory and someone else has to finish the work.

In the Bible, King David got all of the materials, architects and plan prepared for the building of the Temple, but God said, 'you can't build it because you are a man of war.' It was His son, Solomon who actually built the Temple of God. I know in King David's heart he would have loved to build the Temple of God because he was a worshipper, constructed instruments, sang songs, and created poetry unto God; but that job of the actual building and completion was someone else's.

Only God is the beginning, the end, the first, the last, and every step in between. On the other hand, there are some people who get to see the entire process from beginning to end, from planting to harvest, and everything in between. It is satisfying. It is an accomplishment. You can stand back, pat yourself on the back or enjoy the fruit of your labor. You completed the vision that God gave you.

Prayer:

Thank you Lord that I am called to build and my prayer is that Lord, let me do it! In Jesus' name. Amen.

NOTES

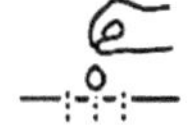

NOTES

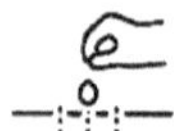

The Prophet's Job

See, I have this day set thee over the nations and over the kingdoms, to root out, and to pull down, and to destroy, and to throw down, to build, and to plant.
Jeremiah 1:10 (KJV)

In the Kingdom, we all have a job to do. We all have somewhere we can serve. We are actually called to serve. There will be a problem — God will call us to do something that we don't want or like to do. Inevitably, someone else will be called to do it, having the grace, anointing, gifts, and talents to do it. These people make it look easy; people are blessed by what they do.

True success is doing exactly what you were born and gifted to do. Jesus said, "For this cause was I born."

Jeremiah had a job to do for God. He didn't like it. He made excuses for not doing it, but God stopped all of his excuses by stating, 'I called you, chose you while you were still in your mother's belly.' No degree, no qualifications, no knowledge, scared, hesitant, feeling some type of way about the assignment — but God still has a job for you to do.

Prayer:

Lord, help me to complete, fulfill and give you glory with the job that you have assigned for me in YOUR Kingdom. In Jesus' name. Amen.

NOTES

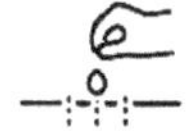

NOTES

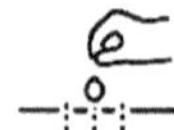

Planted and Rooted

Thou hast planted them, yea, they have taken root: they grow, yea, they bring forth fruit: thou art near in their mouth, and far from their reins.

Jeremiah 12:2 (KJV)

In my home church they often used the phrase, 'I want to be rooted and grounded in God.' Honestly, I was a child and didn't really know what that meant. I was a suburban kid. I was reading books. I was watching other kids play in the streets, shoot basketballs and race each other. Planting what? Not me.

Now, when I went to school, there were Science projects that helped me understand being rooted. The plant was in a clear cup of water so we could all see the roots growing down and the top sprouted up.

After so long, the plant had to be put in dark, brown dirt and we could no longer see anything but the green top kept growing higher and higher in the plastic container.

Planted means to me that He chose me and took the time to gently plant me down in the dirt. After the seed is planted, watered, and given time, it gains roots. If there are no roots in the water, you stay longer in the water. You cannot go to dirt without roots. Once you get roots, you can be planted in dirt. Your roots will grow larger and longer until there will be a season when you outgrow a container, city, or people, and must be uprooted again for bigger opportunities and room to grow deeper and taller.

Prayer:

Thank you God that I am planted and rooted in you. In Jesus' name. Amen.

NOTES

NOTES

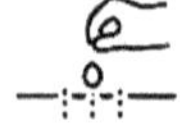

Evil Plants

For the Lord of hosts, that **plant**ed thee, hath pronounced evil against thee, for the evil of the house of Israel and of the house of Judah, which they have done against themselves to provoke me to anger in offering incense unto Baal.

Jeremiah 11:17 (KJV)

Who knew that plants could be evil? They have no personality, right? I don't know what happened in this scripture. The Lord of Hosts did the planting. The children of Israel had done evil and sinned against Jehovah, and the Lord pronounced evil against them. He planted them and they still did evil? How is that possible? Why would you do that? It wasn't an outsider or someone who did not know the ways of Jehovah. What God planted Himself turned to evil.

The children of Israel had to suffer the anger and wrath of God because they did wrong against HIM. God is still sovereign.

He asks no one for their opinion or help in making the decision. Our hope is that we change, repent, turn from those wicked ways and head in the God ordained direction for our lives.

We all have deep within us the ability to sin, do wrong, or serve something that is NOT of God. BUT thankfully, we have the Holy Spirit to change, repent and give us power to do the right thing.

Prayer:

God, give me the power to say yes to YOUR will and no to anything that provokes YOU to anger. In Jesus' name. Amen.

NOTES

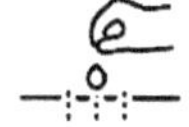

NOTES

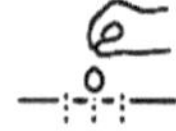

Soil Matters

It was **plant**ed in a good soil by great waters, that it might bring forth branches, and that it might bear fruit, that it might be a goodly vine.

Ezekiel 17:8 (KJV)

For a non-agricultural person like me, it all looks like dirt. There are different colors to the dirt like red dirt, brown dirt, dark almost black dirt but to me it's all dirt.

But to the trained, experienced and wise eye, there is a vast difference in the dirt that certain seeds are planted in. To an expert, it is the difference between a good crop and bad crop. The difference between an abundant harvest and the loss of everything planted for the season. The old Jackson 5 song says, "One bad apple can spoil the whole bunch..." The right seed in the wrong soil or dirt can spoil everything that you are trying to grow. But put the right seed in the right soil, near water and sunlight, drive out the bugs and the worms that seek to eat up your dream — sorry, I mean your crop — before it even gets going, and you will eventually have a harvest.

Be careful where you plant. Let God do the planting because He DOES know the right soil and where the water is.

Prayer:

God, keep me planted me in the right soil. In Jesus' name. Amen.

NOTES

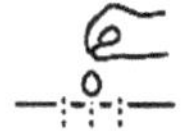

NOTES

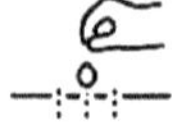

Planted High Enough to See Home

In the mountain of the height of Israel will I **plant** it:

Ezekiel 17:23 (KJV)

There are some things from childhood, home and your family root system that you should never forget. Even the embarrassing mistakes, corrections, and discipline that you remember and thought you'd never get over — you should not forget them. People even bring up some things you did on holidays or at the worst time, in front of people who weren't even there or don't know the context of the situation. But this is all part of life. Good, bad and ugly experiences make you who you are. Mold the person that is still growing and as an adult, those roots go with you no matter where you are.

You may be planted in a totally different environment, people and culture but in your mind, you can still see home.

For Israel, they were planted on a mountain so that they could see home. For you, you see home in your mind — through old photos and text messages. You see home through the smells, food and clothing that you wore or still try to wear even to this day. The saying, 'Home is where the heart is,' is true, but home and what was planted in you is a reflection in the mirror that you see every single day.

Prayer:

Lord, thank you for planting me in spite of, because of and what is unforgettable about home. In Jesus' name. Amen.

NOTES

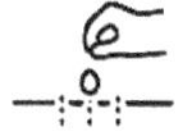

NOTES

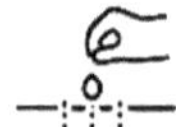

Planted But Wouldn't Stay Put

Ephraim, as I saw Tyrus, is planted in a pleasant place: but Ephraim shall bring forth his children to the murderer.

Hosea 9:13 (KJV)

"The way they act, it's like they were not raised in the same house as the rest of us." Have you ever heard this sentence, phrase, or something similar? Often siblings tease each other by saying, 'they must have switched babies at birth and we got somebody else.' We chuckle but some characteristics and behaviors do not align with the teachings and upbringing in the house. We can be independent, have a 'mind of our own,' and sometimes walk a different path, but a different path than serving God in Israel was not tolerated and was unthinkable. The disrespect, the disobedience and the risk of the consequences were unheard of. Grace and mercy only last so long, and eventually you will pay.

What happens next? The future is at risk. The next generation suffers and your legacy is in jeopardy. You were planted in good soil and by the ultimate God, but you wandered off and chased after what doesn't satisfy — for what? Your future? Go back to where God planted you and stay.

Prayer:

Lord, help me to stay planted in what you called for me no matter the sacrifice because YOUR purpose is what's best for me. In Jesus' name. Amen.

NOTES

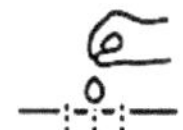

NOTES

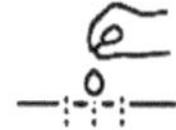

ROOT UP: Not Planted by GOD

But he answered and said, Every **plant**, which my heavenly Father hath not **plant**ed, shall be rooted up.

Matthew 15:13 (KJV)

Some people plant weeds or other plants to kill or deny sunlight and nutrients — through doubt, fear, and a hundred ways — so that something won't grow. Being planted is spiritual. In Matthew it states, anything that the heavenly Father didn't plant needs to be rooted up. Why?

First, He knows the plan for the plant.

Secondly, He knows the complete purpose for the plant to even be planted.

Thirdly, He knows where and what type of soil is best for this particular plant.

Anything that is not planted with His purpose in mind and for YOUR best interest has the potential for misuse, manipulation, and abuse. Thus, eventually, over time, and if you submit to God's will, you'll be rooted up and moved to the soil and situation that best suits your gifts, abilities, and HIS purpose.

If He didn't plant it, it will be rooted up.

Prayer:

Lord, root up anything around me that's not from YOU including me. In Jesus' name. Amen.

NOTES

NOTES

What Did You Plant?

I have planted....

1 Corinthians 3:6 (KJV)

When my husband and I travel, I often see plants in different stages of growth. Sometimes there is nothing visible on the topsoil — just dirt. There are visible neat rows, but nothing has cracked the surface. We can't always see what's first planted unless we put the seed in the ground.

Over time, when we've ventured down this same stretch of highway a month or so later, we see visible signs of growth. Even much later, we can see what is growing in particular fields. I can't tell right away, but my husband will know. He'll say, "That's soybeans or corn, etc." He didn't do the planting, but by what is coming up, he knows what was planted.

What did you plant? Whatever that is, we'll know when it comes up. We'll know what's planted when it comes out of you, too. We'll know by your actions, how you talk, who you are associated with, and how you connect your life.

Be careful. Trust God with what you're planting. Listen to His voice and plant what He intends for you and your life. There is nothing worse than fighting for years for — or about — something that could have been avoided if you had listened and obeyed His voice.

What did you plant?

Prayer:

Lord, help me to plant what you intend for my life. In Jesus' name. Amen.

NOTES

NOTES

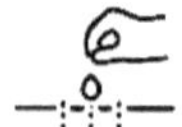

About the Author

Julia Royston spends her days doing what she loves, writing, publishing, speaking about her why and motto, "Helping You Get Your Message to the Masses, Turn Your Words into Wealth and Be a Book Business Boss." Julia is the author of 150+ books, published 500+, recorded 3 music CDs and coached others to be published authors and business owners. She is the owner of five companies, a non-profit organization and the editor of the Book Business Boss Magazine.

To stay connected with Julia, visit www.juliaakroyston.com.

What's Next?

COMING SOON!

Book #2 and Book #3

Devotionals in the Series

Plant. Water. Increase.

Other Books by Julia A Royston

PRODUCT CREATION
PLANNER
WRITE THAT BOOK Now
WRITE THAT BOOK Now WORKBOOK
PROMOTE THAT BOOK Now
PROMOTE THAT BOOK
Julia Royston Books
www.roystonroyalbookstore.com
SONGBOOK
Queen
Queen JOURNAL
IDEA
CREATE
Church BUSINESS
TELLING OUR STORIES

ASK
Julia A. Royston
SEEK
Julia A. Royston
KNOCK
VENDORS AND EXHIBITORS WANTED!
JULIA A. ROYSTON
VENDORS AND EXHIBITORS WANTED!
JULIA A. ROYSTON
ASK
Julia A. Royston
Julia A. Royston
WRITE THE BOOK
JOURNEYS OF FAITH
ECHOES OF FAITH
MINDSET MOVES MOMENTUM
Blessings. Peace. Safety.
Julia A. Royston
Blessings. Peace. Safety.
TRACKED
ARE YOU MEDIA READY?
PLANS ACTIONS GO!
Speaking About and From Your Book
Review Prepare Execute
Julia A. Royston
Social Media for Authors and Business Owners
Julia A. Royston
Coming Soon!
WRITE THAT BOOK Now 2.0
Coming Soon!
PUBLISH THAT BOOK
Coming Soon!
PROMOTE THAT BOOK Now 2.0
Coming Soon!
TRACKED 2
Julia Royston Books
www.roystonroyalbookstore.com

www.ingramcontent.com/pod-product-compliance
Lightning Source LLC
LaVergne TN
LVHW010938110826
845149LV00013B/2661

* 9 7 8 1 9 7 1 8 6 8 3 0 1 *